leaves of water

RALPH WRIGHT, O.S.B.

[signature: Ralph Wright O.S.B.]

leaves of water

new & selected poems

Saint Louis Abbey Press

Saint Louis, Missouri

Library of Congress
Catalog Card Number 97-091336
ISBN 0-9662104-0-9

Printed in the United States of America

DEDICATION

For Anne Porter
whose 'altogether different language'
has reminded me
that poetry is
above all
memorable speech.

ACKNOWLEDGEMENTS

I would like to thank the Daughters of Saint Paul for permission to include the poems "Today", "Ripples of Stillness", "Ground for Joy" and "Infinite Patience" which first appeared in a collection of my poetry that they published entitled *Ripples of Stillness.*

I am deeply grateful to Stan Gellman who designed the cover. My thanks also to Cumming and Cleda Paton and Joann Harvey without whom this project would never have got off the ground.

CONTENTS

New Poems
1993–1997

Words, after speech, reach into the silence.

T.S.Eliot

NEW POEMS

1993–1997

leaves of water

I wonder did
   God think of leaves
     falling from
       the autumn trees

before he thought
   of flakes of snow
     leaves of water
       drifting so

gently in
   December's breeze
     they might have been
       October's leaves

Canada Geese

Canada geese
lumbering nobly along
grazing
in strict formation
their long black necks
poking
like vacuum cleaners
at the winter grass

one at the back
erect
tall as a watch tower
with both eyes and a beak
steady
alert for danger

stately as a squadron
in the Pacific
parading before Mountbatten
cropping
chewing
digesting
dunging the pathways

and then
at a nod from the tower
aloft instantly

cruising more smoothly
over the grey and the blue
than over the green

Thwack

walking between
the dark green
heavy plastic
end curtains
and the stark wall
in the Indoor Tennis
Club last night
as the heavy popping
thud of racket
striking ball
hit my ears
I suddenly wondered
why the relatively
sane men and
saner women
from Homer's day
down to our own
have whiled away
with such relish
endless hours
thwacking or watching
others thwack
a bland ball

unless it's because
we're genetically bound
to mirror our Father
whose glorious
mischievous
somehow superfluous
always mysterious

cosmic game
we
now
eternally
are

In the Murk

In the murk
of day by day
tragic being
some people
reach for a way
to end their prolonged
darkness

others have seen
and remember
the signs of dawn
appearing on the fringes
of the long night sky

others stay around
from a kind of curiosity
to see what'll happen
next

today
I find myself rooted
to the spot
— fiddle beneath my chin
bow poised —
waiting
after last night's interval
for the conductor's raised hand
and the momentary silence
before the new movement
begins

In Your Light We See Light[1]

"...in your light we see light."
as darkness falls over the silent
steady fall of this relentless snow;

"...in *your* light..."
the meaning of it all
the sudden comfort coming from deep awareness
that You exist and I am loved by You —
a blanket of quiet hope to ease the mind
reducing the angry roar of torn nerves
to silence;

"...your *light*..."
the Spirit simply dwelling in the deep
focal point of the person that I am,
dwelling like blazing logs in the wood stove
against the backdrop of the wild
zero winter night;

"...we see light."
but not the light
that dissipates the wonder of the world
into a billion facts and references;
not the light
of geiger counter, meter and statistic
reducing all
to the probability of ten decimal places;
nor even the light of deconstructionism
analysing
with all the subtlety of the pathologist,

taking the tissue from the one deceased
to track the dread disease
but leaving Beauty hunched like a morgue cadaver
cold on the marble table of the mind;

"…we see light."
the light of stunned wonder overwhelmed
reeling from too much glory;
the light that seems a healing from great blindness
as if we were born an adult and saw
at once unveiled like a new statue
all of the mystery in created being;

the light that knows itself
able to love and long beloved by You;
the light that sees all suffering
as privilege offered sparingly by Christ
to those chosen from all eternity
to share in the immense undertaking
of forging Man's reunion with God –

this God in whose great fountainhead of light
we now see
the snow that still comes silent from the sky
relentless in its careful long caress
as this long night gives way
and the mute darkness is diluted
gradually to the white and muted grey
of another winter dawn.

---

[1] Psalm 35.10

Tongued with Fire

God spoke
to Moses
on the mountain
and his words
were carved
on tablets
of stone

when the Son of Man
wrote
we are told
he wrote
with his finger
in the sand

what he wrote
in the sand
no one knows
— it blew
like dust
in the wind

but the fire
he lit
on the mountain
still roars
in the mind

our sins

our sins
do not
make God
love us less
but more
because
our need is greater

If Words

if words
were my medium
I would tell
what lies behind
our silences
as your gaze
brings joy and laughter
to my heart

smoke
rising
from the Black Hills
against
a sunset sky

August

the first small leaves
of maple trees
are falling
through the shade
towards the yet
uncovered ground
and as they fall
I see them for
they twice hit sunlight

You Glove the Light

You glove the light
before it scorch the mind
and so we move
in corridors of gloom
searching for meaning

why darken brilliance
from dust to raindrops
when we are so athirst
for drafts of pure amazement

and eager to applaud
even the spider on the wall
the low complaining bullfrog on the pond
and the Canadian geese
against the blueberry night
forming an eloquent V

A Young Willow Fountain of Ice

A young willow fountain of ice
this morning after Matins
against a rose January sky—
a masterpiece of curves in crystal
of haunting mauve beauty

blending the essentially gentle
giving receiving circle of compassion
with the straight brittle seize and take
battle line of ultimata—
the Yes or No intransigence
of arrogance

an angry impatience
at the evil
in every heart even our own
that leaves a litany
of booted limbs
protruding from
Napoleonic snow

The Story of Time

the story of time is told in every leaf
the blending mooded spectrum of them all
needing the drumming open stage of time
to conjugate the splendor of their being

those like us with mind might need only
instants to say 'Yes' and to be whole
like spirits on a needlehead of 'No'
but leaves require the pageantry of Fall
to dance their glory down into the grime

If You Are Made

if you are made
Man
by God
to share his life
then nothing
They may say
or do
can ever reduce
the barely finite
grandeur
of your being

It Took All the Chemistry

it took all the chemistry
since Big Bang
to pedigree
the DNA
union
that is 'me'

that's one
huge
mind-defying
History
— Heap Big Mystery

the answer to all harmony is seeing
that this is not just inconceivable
but true

and for 'you' too!

If God

If God
had been
indifferent
to you
he'd
have made
someone else

When You Receive

when you receive
    your invitation
        to the Feast
           of the Lamb

be at peace
    undismayed
        for this
           you were made

Every Word Spoken

every
word
spoken
is
as
past
as
pyramids
and
gone
forever

Among the Gentiles

but with you
it must not be so
for it is not so
with Me

Bethlehem
Nazareth
Gethsemane
where
as people minded their sheep
the galaxy
was repoured

and St. Louis
where
this noon
as you came in
out of the cold
a Star of David snowflake
on your sleeve
before it melted
perfectly
told all

Incompetence

because You are Love
therefore are You incompetent
therefore are You unable
to abolish war
or hatred
or hunger
or even indifference

if You had been Power
what a tidy
cosy
computerized
universe it would be
but how cold and empty
the spaces between the stars

Scripture

from the silicon chip
that spawned a myriad
galaxies of immediate
information

and the DNA
genetic code
that at conception
casts in concrete
a billion messages
for our construction

we may read Your glory
just as clearly
as in the larger
scripture of the heavens

where pinpoints of light
riding the infinite
empty spaces
provide
for the unclouded mind
on a moonless night
more than enough for wonder

Souvenir

through the long slit window
I watched the branches move
up and down
up and down
as though a squirrel
out of sight
had landed on one
or leapt from one
or as though a bird
beyond my vision
had alighted
or taken off
in the frozen air

soon the limbs
were still again

how long will I remember
seeing the branches move?

Since Babel God

Since Babel God
spoke haltingly
through prophets
(whom we killed)
down to our own
sweet day

when
to avoid
the ambiguities
of language
God sent in flesh his Son

this flesh
we nailed
like incoherence
to a tree

but he
rose to win us wholeness
making all twos one
unbabeling our language
in the blood of union

Galilee

Dusk light burns golden on the water
while six-inch waves break lightly on the shore.
The divers and the cormorants
glide among protruding trees
and the whole scene speaks of paradise.

For here you walked and talked
and healed and called
multitudes of people
out of the loneliness of petty hatreds
to the one family of your Father
and into untold union within you.

But even the dusk and quiet light
and these sweet memories cannot conceal
the travesties of human love that still
trick our hearts and multiply our hungers
with this strange constant need to be supreme.

Yet here could we not say, and then let silence speak,
'Now tragedy may never be complete.' ?

Words Happen To You

words happen to you
like daybreak or flu

through no fault of yours
words are your applause

labyrinth, mausoleum,
or Red Woods at dawn
words are your medium
to mitigate gloom

In Memory of My Mother

One day I will write of you feather-light words
that will bring you back to me laughing and strong
wild on the air with warmth and comfort
fighting with wisdom and care—
one day I will write of you hardly with words
wet on the tip of my pen but not here
now at this moment now is too near
you are too near to me distance is needed
if I am to write somehow essentially
words about you—
so now I must wait but one day I'll write
before your face your smile and your tenderness
leap too far from my view
when you have become somehow more apart from me
and I have received new calm
I will poise on the air snow-lilting words
dancing aspects of you.

Guy
— *a memory*

Beeley the morning mist and grouse
complaining against aggression
welsh laughter partridges and trout
and Cherry Brandy
moments of cricket sunshine clapping warmth
and a carefree
calm and relaxed enjoyment life being there
given surely above all by God
to be lived, loved and laughed by
how clear is the memory of a man
we loved, lived and laughed with
is there a single call that now
can
somehow
echo our loss
'Joss come here
come here Joss
Joss *will* you come here
Joss...'

John Wayne

with that look in the eye
that reflected
the eternal hills
we watched you
nonchalantly
stare down evil
and
with that strange blend
of
Robin Hood
Sherlock Holmes
and
Batman
blow it away
with both hands blazing

London Interior

in the fifteen minutes'
pause
between trains
two pigeons
shoulder to shoulder
march towards me
on the platform
at Victoria Station
like grenadiers

they divide
and peck adroitly
at potential food

the platform
is so polished
that as they peck
they kiss
their reflection

SELECTED POEMS

1978–1992

Today

Today
I will do nothing
but grow
older
and so draw
nearer
to the moment
of eternal union
with you —
how wonderful
to achieve so much
by doing nothing

Ripples of Stillness

God threw a rock the other day
— His Word —
gently
into the wild pool of His creation

—

ripples of stillness
are still widening
towards the shore

Ground For Joy

My past lies
in the merciful hands of God
my future
in His wise love
the present moment
in which I live
is of no duration
how then may fear win
mastery over my joy?

Infinite Patience

God lets
his Son
be stretched
against
the earth
and nailed
to the wood
of the world
behold
the mystery
of infinite
patience
that
God
should create
a being
able
to see
and love
or blindly
hate
then patiently
wait
and not
stop
the entire
show
when an innocent
child
weeps in the
night

or his Son
is stretched
against
the world
and brutally
nailed

People Whisper God to Me

People whisper God to me
far more than mountains
for landscape beauty bores —
however roaring or majestic
is the pageant music
played behind
their massive faces
sunsets have no sympathy
and — for all its background
awe-inspiring paintwash —
granite cannot smile.

I Will Write of Moments

I will write of moments
tasted together — new wine —
to a background of confident
rhythmical stark 'griechische Musik'
untouched by dreams.
I will write in thanks
for the simple joy
of finding a friend
whom — if I were God —
I would have created.
I will write of what must remain
forever wordless
— thoughts
caught in the frail
net of the intellect —
for only the heart
really can tell
(but cannot being tongueless)
of what I am writing —
and writing now
before the snow falls
and the slow song of autumn
dies in the distance
and before this moment
is lost in the sunlight
the misted sunlight
of smouldering leaves —
and now I have said
almost nothing
and it is written.

A Poem for Judy

reading your poems I am aware of wine
constrained in a cask within the dark
cellar of your heart

a wine won from a chosen vintage
— grapes that hung in full sunlight
until they were ripe for treading —

a wine mellowing through the years of silence
towards an appointed glory in the glass

The Shadow of the Wind

I have seen with you
the shadow of the wind
thrown by tall trees
guarding the dark water
the shadow of the wind
keeping a certain calm
against the constant turbulence
of changing light and darkness
I have seen in you and known
the shadow of the wind
as clouds race white and black
across the sky
and in this calm I found
a joy that cannot fear
what dark may do to me beyond
the shadow of the wind.

Warshock
on looking at a picture in the Pentagon

wide eyes
stare
out of nobody
into nothing

shell burst
mind burst
blind

like surf
men break
endlessly
on this beach

rippling the sand

Swallow

With a lightning dive and a
swoop
sweeping long and low
over rolling grass, hillside
and sudden pools
skimming the ground or the water and swinging
with boomerang motion
back and high in the air
handsome as Hector and sleek
as some Black Beauty
groomed stud stallion
— only for speed —
you knive your way
through empty air
with scimitar sureness
and finite ease
leaving a wake
of high peep notes
and with the passing
pen of your passage
writing beauty
alive in the sky

Birthday Utterance

I have great joy
in knowing that you
have been
born
into the world
because
having been breathed
by God
into existence
you will never
be able
— like a bubble —
to pop
suddenly
back into nothingness

welcome
to this one great
champagne
dancing
party of being

and be
always
alive and utterly
grateful to Him
who
simply freely spontaneously
needlessly and
eternally
utters

Occurrence

You might have been born in Hong Kong
when Ghengis Khan
was pounding the planet.
Or even today, aeons away,
in London or Tokyo.
But somehow someone's kindly computer
decided
that you should be
roughly here
roughly now
and with four thousand million
currently elsewhere
I almost explode
with thanksgiving
as I blunder
like some beautiful rhino
casually out of the bush
into the path of your being.

Rose

from folded bud
to open bloom
you move like royalty
knowing yourself adored

accepting from
the silence of the dawn
your sole applause
you move
from youth towards magnificence
while the proud mates
of potentates
for dignity
borrow your fragrance

your colors are
the arbiters of excellence
all bow
before your being

when the symphony is over
and you die
Eden is empty

Leaf Fall

I was not watching but I heard
a leaf fall off an indoor plant just now
and hit the carpet in the perfect stillness —
as it fell it touched another leaf
and so I heard its fall —
there was no kind of wind or other force
to cause this brief event, it seems it fell
simply because it had been growing
silently old long enough
to earn this parting —
it may be at least a week or even a month
before another leaf from the same plant
merits this moment
so what a simple grace and gift it was,
and quite uncalled for,
to be there at this instant not to watch
— as one might watch a lift-off towards the moon —
but, as befits its call to be discreet,
only to hear the falling of this leaf.

If Death

if death
is not
the doorway to life
then I
am just
a superior leaf
hanging a season
out of the sky
then falling briefly
into the earth
small manure
barely enough
to properly dung a rose with

Messiah

anoint the wounds
of my spirit
with the balm
of forgiveness
pour the oil
of your calm
on the waters
of my heart

take the squeal
of frustration
from the wheels
of my passion
that the power
of your tenderness
may smooth
the way I love

that the tedium
of giving
in the risk
of surrender
and the reaching
out naked
to a world
that must wound

may be kindled
fresh daily
to a blaze
of compassion

that the grain
may fall gladly
to burst in the ground
— and the harvest abound

People Tell Me

People tell me "Don't be afraid of God,
for God is Love."
O don't you see
I fear the very Lover
in my God!

I fear the Lover
hiding glory in the drab disguise
of humble people

I fear the Lover
barely daring to reveal
his gentle breeze of being
lest majesty beget
tremendous homage

I fear the one who loves me
and touches with such tenderness
this fragile thing of freedom that is "me"
lest it be shattered

and yet perhaps I have no fear of God
but of his being Love
and so of me

I fear the fact that he is Love and so
must leave me all the drama of decision
that love requires
                as sure as light reveals
and darkness veils, I too must choose
the narrow way, the holocaust, the bleak

leap of abandonment into the barely known
and yet demanding deep —
I fear the fact that I am made to choose
and so may lose

Life is Simpler Towards Evening

life is simpler towards evening
shadows longer quieter
and more complete
things are calm

we no longer throttle speech
from mystery
but having lived through long years
respect silence

we no longer audit God's accounts
with the same agony
but knowing him more deeply know that he
is good for loving

now vision comes
only in lightning
leaving us blinder than before
but more aware
that change remains our permanent despair

pulled by a current out of our control
we live in a growing past
the myth of happiness stains our empty glass
time corks the joy of every swift delight
but moments test the passing wine
and find in it a tang of the eternal

Cana

there was far
too much wine
at Cana
for there to be no laughter

and Jesus added to it

Befuddled

A slow befuddled winter fly
 with 747 abandon
has trundled from my window sill
 and God knows what he'll land on.

Such geriatric flies present
 a crisis to compassion:
to smear them or to leave them space
 to die in their own fashion.

being older

being older
is being conscious
of being bones

posing the question
as right and proper
of the dust doorway
with the skull knocker

daring to plunge
in thoughts of void
or kingdom come

being older
is tasting life
with a new tongue
knowing the sap
will fail to run

seeing new
touching new
loving new

and being bolder
for being bones

When God Made You

When
God
made
you
there
was
silence
in
heaven
for
five
minutes.
Then
God
said
"How come I never thought of *that* before?"

Through a Glass Darkly

only a thin
film of glass
protects the moth
as it bangs
again and again
against the light
in the dark night
from the sizzle
of extinction

Conceive

to bring
    and to have brought
into being
    through God

one called
    to live forever
intimately
    with God

what a stunning
    mind-scalding
thing to do
    and to have done

could anything
    conceivably
be greater —
    none

The Big Myth Is That
There's Too Little Light

The big myth is that there's too little light
for us to see by — but there's far too much.
The shadows from small gravel in the dusk,
the magic and magnificence of seasons,
or leaves turning from green to gold to rust —
are all too full of the mind of the Creator,
they leave us blinded and absorbed by dust.

Dust is our medium and we mold it firm
to build a plastic heart and reach the moon.
Things have become idols and our minds
feed on distractions leaving little room
for silence or monogamy in prayer.
Someone has opened the camera to expose
our vision to the swift assault of light.
All of our wonder is being drowned by dust.
O not too little light but far too much.

From All Eternity

from all eternity
You made me
as if to be
your only spouse
in time
may I choose You
to be mine

Jericho

The man who fell in with thieves
on his way to Jericho
may have been going there
— for all we know —
to murder his mother

he may have come
from robbing the Temple
or sleeping with his next-door-neighbor's wife
— we are not told —

the man who finds him
half-dead
clearly does not know

and God seems to be hammering home
blow by blow
the thought
that worthiness is irrelevant

all we need
is to recognize need

Theophany

A fine dry
stalk structure
on which are poised
with total symmetry
tiny wind-blown
toy umbrellas
forming a perfect
Fabergé sphere —
a Czar's jewel
beyond fury
good for nothing
but reflecting glory—
Yellow Goatsbeard,
a dead weed
ripe
for launching seed.

The Birds

the birds
make all
worth while

singing us
out of our
drab tragedies

into
a new
world

of sunrise
springtime
grace
and movement

a ballet
of
exuberance

before the silence
of winter
leaves only

a few
crumbs
scattered

in the omnipotent
wide
snow

Out of a Deep

out of a deep
respect for silence
a poet speaks
without violence

he speaks to be heard
below the noise
with a quiet voice
but without reserve

not with the agony
of a Laocoon
struggling with snakes
for articulation

but with playful
hands that feel
his words like clay
on a potter's wheel

he accepts the gentle
humiliation
of time and space
in anticipation

of the final moment
of eternal union
beyond music
beyond illusion

Great Calm

I am filled with joy
that God loves you
with great competence
for my love is infinite
in clumsiness—
when I wound
He heals
when I damage
He restores
and you are always
in his hands
O great calm
O mighty God
O quiet joy

The Godmaker

within the tightened nutshell of my mind
where I pretend to godhead
I make God
after my own image
God Who Is
impervious to all
the adumbrations of my wild desires
beyond before bestriding
without thought
the cataracting galaxies of years
I make an idol and ignore
the image given
and refuse
to let God be the kind of god who gives
the elbow-room I need for being wild
the kind of god who chooses to know wounds
and emptiness in place of full delight
the kind of god some dare to think prefers
— after so many aeons of instant being —
to make a batch of things that fail a while
and leave them space and time in which to heal

O Hidden God

God finds it such a business staying hidden
with ski-masks, plastic gloves and moving
around only when all are drunk
or simply sleeping
he has to be so sure to leave no trace
though sometimes in his carelessness he leaves
a kind of jet-wake in a sunset sky
or something like the slime a slug expels
to help its passage on a blade of grass
but mostly people overlook these clues —

If he should quit this game of hide-and-seek
— as often in our ire we tell him to —
and let himself be caught red-handed
selecting this one sperm for this one egg
or breathing the odd galaxy into being
what space for fun and laughter could remain?
we'd all have ulcers or be dead for awe.

Unsurprised by Darkness

if God's own Son
had to brink despair
dying in the darkness
of noonday night

why should I
know a tranquil passage
from finite groping
to infinite Light

why am I shocked
by the daily trauma
woven into
the heart of flesh

the rending anger
perdures from the womb
till the hands are folded
in the calm of death

see the stars
and ponder the Word
in whom each galaxy
finds its being

then watch the one
whose humble coming
respects the measure
of our seeing

for "who can live
with a blazing fire?"
O mercifully mercifully
hidden God

coming as breeze
coming as bread
coming through the grape
our feet have trod

I Listened to the Sound of Rain

I listened to the sound of rain
upon the leaves
approaching with the wind
—— the rain and wind were still some woods away

I listened to the terror of the wind
upon the leaves in anger tearing them
untimely out of life and swirling them
at random in the dark upon the ground

I listened to the calm that came
from nowhere on the leaves
when suddenly the angry air was gone
I heard them welcome with relief
the newborn silence of the night
and watch in awe for dawn

Seamless

Stretched between tall grass in the dawn light
the cobweb shimmers—
rainbows,
magic innocence,
routine evil.

The fighters with folded wings
stand at parade as the carrier moves
through mediterranean blue,
inspected annually by the Queen
an admiral at each elbow.

Even the spider moves like a priest
towards his breakfast sacrifice,
but how does the fly feel
caught on the wire
before and after the jaws?

I sat at the back of the church.
Under the dome a spider hung
caught like a copter in the sun.
A tiny lump of gold it soared and plunged,
soared and plunged.
A trapeze artist high in the Big Top.
A secretary typing a routine letter
in total silence.
A seamstress mending a torn and seamless robe.

St. Louis. Freezing Rain. Postlude.

The icicles are trees this morning
in crystal wonderlands that burst the heart
all the Fabergés of every art
since cave men sketched their bison on the walls
are children building castles on the sand
compared to these ——
twigs and limbs with every hang of ice
poise paradise in filaments of light
splintered through a million perfect prisms
throwing a circuit-breaker in our heads
lest overload should burn away the mind
and leave us foolish

and yet You chose in wisdom to forego
this icescape ecstasy when You came
to live a lifetime here so long ago
if You had come to Palestine today
You could yourself have seen with your own eyes
this sparkle kingdom that was gone by noon
with your own eyes You could yourself have seen
and then been
back at the Beautiful Gate for evening prayer
by special Concorde via Tel Aviv
to hear the bombs go off and drink the wine
and see the sun go down and yet You chose
to see it all through mine.

In Memory of Graham

I dreamt the night was clear and just outside
some kind of hut or house I saw the sky
clearer than I had ever gazed at it before,
with the astronomer's Horse and Bear
now for the first time easy to be seen,
like number points rimming a child's drawing
at last without the guesswork needed
from all my wild imagining.

Each star a sun to raise a world at dawn
and bed the whole thing down again at night.

It blew my mind away to think of God
at ease with such immensity as this
receiving you, my friend, into eternity
and planning even now a place for me.
That God who works so large can love so small!
That God who thinks in billions could become
on this brief atom earth so few as one!

Dogma

the thin
finite
confining
walls
of a tall glass
enable
infinite
water
to reach
thirsty lips

It's Dangerous to Be Me

It's dangerous to be me today
it's dangerous — can't you see?
Be glad you're someone else today
someone who isn't me.

I'm wild and high and raging glad,
I'm more than half-way free.
O keep away and be yourself —
it's dangerous to be me.

It's dangerous to be me today
for being almost free
I've told it like it is today
and never feared the knee.

I've raged at all hypocrisy.
I've scorned all compromise.
I've glimpsed each person's dignity
as if through God's own eyes.

It's dangerous to be me today
maybe tomorrow too.
O come be wild with me until
it's dangerous to be you!

You Are So Everywhere

You are so everywhere
at times
that the mind
puts on shades
to polaroid the glare

at times You are so nowhere
that even the blazing
noonday naked sun
parching the almost naked
bodies on the beach
brown for pretended glamor
blares only emptiness
into the hallway
of my heart

but usually
You are so everywhere
one moment
and so gone the next
like grasshoppers
clinging to stalks
of Shepherd's Beard
seeming
totally still
but priming a whisker
here or there
for instant take-off

how far d'you think they'd leap upon the moon?

A New Terror

if I may only be forgiven
if I forgive
I should tremble
at the hardness
of my heart
and quake
more radically
at the intransigence
of your compassion

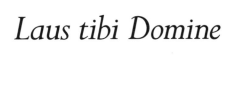

Laus tibi Domine

Ralph Wright, O.S.B. was born in
England in 1938. He received his early
education at Ampleforth College in
Yorkshire, England and is a Benedictine
monk at Saint Louis Abbey in Saint
Louis, Missouri.

Wright is a poet of great distinction
whose work reflects his knowledge of
and respect for the masters. His images
are both beautiful and startling; his
metaphors perceptive, his use of rhyme
natural. Wright's expertise lies in
the unity of word and idea that is the
essence of poetry. *Leaves of water* is his
sixth book of verse.